TEE'D OFF

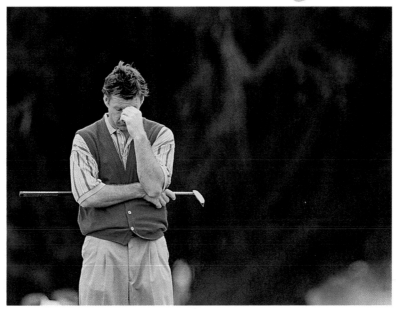

First published in Great Britain in 1999 by

Chameleon Books

76 Dean Street

London W1V 5HA

Copyright for text © Generation Publications Ltd

CIP data for this title is available from the British Library

ISBN 0 233 99500 5

Book and jacket design by Generation Studio

Reprographics by Jade Reprographics

Printed in Spain

ACKNOWLEDGEMENTS:

Also a special thanks to Dave Crowe, Eddie Schillace,

Paul Sudbury, Linda Baritski, Caroline Warde, Eve Cossins, Mark Peacock,

Mary Killingworth, Joe Crowe, Louise Dixon and Tim Forrester.

PHOTOGRAPH ACKNOWLEDGEMENTS

All Photographs supplied by Allsport U.K LTD.

Dedicated To : Hackers everywhere

"Silly trousers, worse shirts, chasing an impossibly small ball around a large field for 4 hours, dodging the club secretary because you've ditched your shirt and tie, mega-expensive clubs that promise ultimate distance if you didn't wield them like a cricket bat, more sand, rain and water than a lousy weekend in Bognor and more foraging in foliage than a tribesman from Borneo - golf, what a game. I love it."

Chris Evans

FITNESS FANATICS

"I hate these bloody flowers".

Swedish player Jesper Parnevik is commonly recognised as one of the game's eccentrics, something which may be a result of him being the son of his country's top comedian. One of Parnevik's habits is to eat volcano dust to help his body cleanse itself of negative feelings.

Britain's young rising stars Darren Clarke and Lee Westwood both found themselves under fire from South African Gary Player, who aimed a dig at the not too slimline figures of Clarke and Westwood, saying they were too fat to win Major Championships. Not long after Westwood became a regular visitor to the European Tour gymnasium.

As a teenager, American LPGA Tour player Kris Tschetter harboured ambitions about making a living out of ballet, but she missed out on succeeding in entry rehearsals for the South Dakota School of Ballet. She instead turned to golf, but 15 years later returned to the ballet to help herself keep supple and fit for life on the professional circuit.

These exploding balls are a pain in the arse.

Jack Nicklaus once went on a diet of **cabbage soup** to help himself stay conditioned for the Tour, a step that moved Tom Watson to remark that he would rather not play downwind of the Golden Bear.

LOTS OF SHOTS

Maurice Flitcroft holds a special place in Open Championship history. A 46-year-old crane driver, Flitcroft entered the qualifying stages of the 1976 Open, despite having never played a round of 18 holes ever before. His golfing experience was mainly limited to practising on his local beach. Flitcroft shot 121 in his first qualifying round at Formby before withdrawing. He said afterwards: "I've made a lot of progress in the last few months and I'm sorry I didn't do better. I was trying too hard at the beginning but began to put things together at the end of the round."

"And when your son grows up, he'll be Davis Love V."

"You must be bloody joking."

Seve playing that all important fifth chip shot onto the first fairway.

An American called Walter Danecki entered The Open in 1965 but never looked likely to make it through qualifying. Playing at the Hillside GC at Southport, Danecki recorded rounds of 108 and 113 to stand at 81-over par for the 36 holes.

In the 1968 French Open, Brian Barnes managed a score of 15 at the short 8th hole at St Cloud, having actually been putting for a four from only about three feet. In frustration at missing a couple of short ones, Barnes managed to pile up a handful of penalty shots as well by hitting the ball while it was still moving, and also standing astride the line of a putt.

Floyd Rood once golfed his way across the breadth of the USA, taking 479 days and using a total of 114,737 shots.

It must a be a rare occasion when a mountain is declared the winner in a golf match but so it was for Ben Nevis in 1961 when four students from Aberdeen decided to see if they could golf their way to the summit. The students conceded defeat at around the halfway point after some 659 shots and a total of 63 lost balls.

At the treacherous par-3 12th hole at Augusta, scene of many heartbreaking moments in the US Masters, Tom Weiskopf managed to run up a score of 13 during the first round of the 1980 tournament. He hit his ball into the water in front of the green no less than five times.

YOU ANIMALS

WJ Robinson, the professional at St Margaret's-at-Cliffe GC in Kent, managed to kill a cow with his tee shot at the 18th hole while playing in June, 1934. The cow was standing 100 yards from the teebox in the fairway when Robertson's ball struck it squarely on the back of the head. The cow fell, regained its feet and staggered 50 yards, then collapsed and died.

After winning the 1998 Bridgestone Open in Japan, Australian player Ian Baker-Finch looked forward to receiving his winner's cheque, and an additional sponsor's bonus. But it must have come as something of a surprise when, instead of the expected gold watch or car, he was presented with a cow - donated by a local farming co-operative.

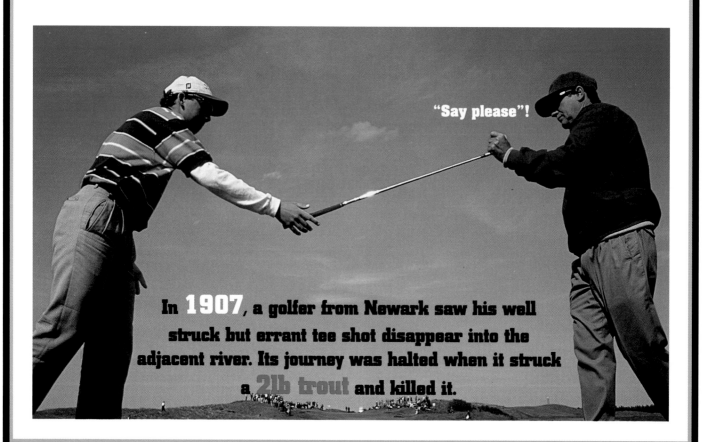

"Say please"!

In 1907, a golfer from Newark saw his well struck but errant tee shot disappear into the adjacent river. Its journey was halted when it struck a 2lb trout and killed it.

"Shan't play faster. I shan't, shan't, shan't!"

Dan McDonald, president of the Lakeside Country Club in Wisconsin, received an unexpected helping hand from a cow when playing his course in 1915. McDonald sliced his opening drive and the ball struck the cow, which had wandered on to the course. Not overly happy at being hit by the ball, the cow kicked out at it and sent it hurtling onto the green. McDonald holed the putt for a birdie.

Waddy, an 11-year-old Beagle belonging to the secretary of Brokenhurst Manor GC, had a nose for finding lost golf **balls**. He collected over **35,000** of them.

In Massachusetts a goose took revenge on a golfer who managed to hit it with a stray shot by walking over to where the ball came to rest and kicking it into the water hazard.

IS GOLF DANGEROUS?

Such is the casualty rate for heat stroke at a desert golf course in Mojave, California, that the club has installed emergency telephones on the fairways for golfers in distress.

Leicester City and USA goalkeeper Kasey Keller has a big gap in his mouth where two front teeth should reside. He lost them not when diving bravely at a centre forward's feet, but when he pulled a golf club out of his bag rather too energetically.

A Japanese sports doctor, Keizo Kogure, has conducted a study in which he concludes that golf is eight times more likely to kill a man over the age of 60 than jogging.

The death rate in golf is, apparently, higher than in mountaineering and Kogure also reckons that some 5,000 people die each year while playing golf in Japan.

Old Elephant Dick hole causing a problem for Ernie.

I sunk one!

Multi storey driving ranges are common in Japan where land is scarce and expensive. But playing from the top tier can be a dangerous pastime, as Toshiaki Yujima found in 1989 when he fell three stories off the range and broke his leg.

Brett Ogle found out the hard way that it pays to check your health insurance is up to date. Playing in the 1990 Australian Open, and lying close to the lead, Ogle tried to thread a long iron through a gap in the trees ahead of him. Instead the ball cannoned into the tree, rebounded back like a rocket, hit Ogle on the leg and broke his kneecap.

Richard McCulough died after playing a poor tee shot at the 13th hole of the Ponoka Community GC in Canada. In anger at his bad drive, McCulough smashed his club against his buggy. The club snapped and the broken shaft severed McCulough's carotid artery - he died in hospital.

Rudolph Roy was killed in bizarre circumstances while playing at a course in Montreal in 1971. Playing a shot out of trees, **Roy's club snapped** and then rebounded off a tree - the sharp end stabbing the unfortunate Roy with fatal consequences.

RULES ARE RULES

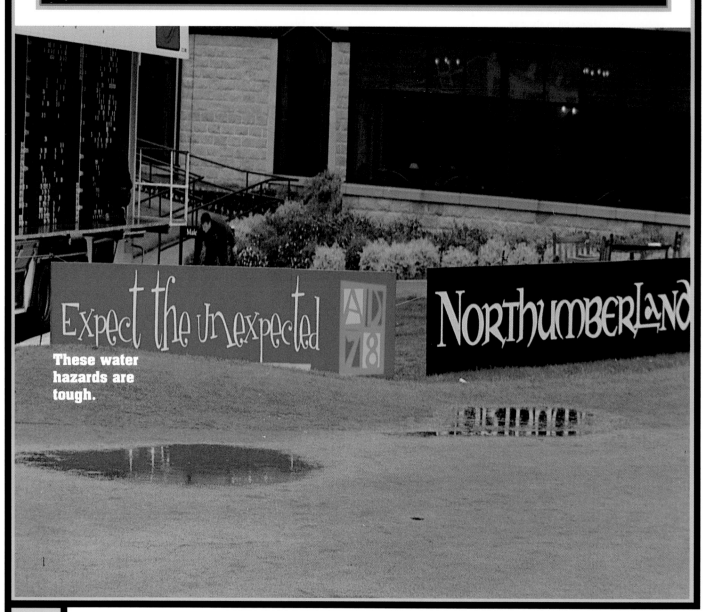

These water hazards are tough.

Ignacio Garrido struggled to find his form during 1998, but it seemed to be coming back at the One 2 One British Masters in September. However, he started a round unaware that one of his practice clubs was still in the bag, and he had one more than the maximum allowed 14. The result he was penalised a total of four shots - and he ended the week just two shots behind the winner Colin Montgomerie.

Ian Woosnam got caught short at a green during the 1991 World Cup of Golf, and nipped off a to a portaloo. Unfortunately in his haste he forgot to mark his ball before picking it up off the green and had to be penalised one shot. Woosnam and his partner representing Wales duly finished second - one shot behind Sweden.

Chip Beck suffered at the hands of the rules during the 1992 Greater Greensboro Open. Tied for the lead playing the 15th in the third round, Beck's wayward tee shot landed next to an out of bounds stake but within the boundaries of the course. Beck eyed up his shot, and to help his stance, pulled the stake out of the ground. Then, thinking he may be breaking a rule, he put it back before playing his shot. Unfortunately, simply moving the stake incurred a penalty of two strokes, which ultimately meant Beck finished third instead of second and received $81,000 less in winnings.

"Golf is not a sport.
Golf is men
in ugly pants,
walking."
Rosie O'Donnell

"Honestly Glenn, Ian and I are both poorly".

Night raider

Australian veteran Dan Cullen, still a fine golfer well into his 80s, also managed to win a few tournaments in his younger days. A wartime flyer of Lancaster bombers out of the UK, one of Cullen's post-war European successes came in a tournament in Germany. When Cullen stepped up to receive his trophy he was asked by the sponsor if he had ever travelled to Germany before, to which Cullen replied: "Only at night."

Soft landing

In contention for the 1968 World Series of Golf, Gary Player pushed his tee shot at the 12th in the final round to the right of the green. The ball was destined for deep trouble until it hit a woman spectator on the chest and lodged between her breasts. The rules official allowed Player to place the ball at the woman's feet and play his next shot from there - he chipped close and made par, eventually going on to win the tournament.

Long ball

At the 1992 Texas Open Carl Cooper managed to hit his tee shot at the 456-yard 3rd hole an amazing 787 yards, which meant he contrived to overshoot the green by some 300+ yards. Cooper's amazing drive made its first bounce on a concrete buggy path before careering down a roadway and finally coming to rest by a fence, which was stood nearly half a mile away from the teebox.

JS Murray was elected captain of Norwich GC in 1973, and with his first ever shot as club captain he scored a hole in one.

There are serious
golfers and not so
serious golfers.

"I don't know who designed the **Road Hole**, but I hear he's escaped."
Mark James

"I am a **great** golfer. I just haven't played the game yet."
Muhammed Ali

Flag day

Playing the par-3 12th hole during the 1936 Irish Open, Bobby Locke's tee shot made a beeline for the pin, but somewhere between the teebox and the pin the ball just seemed to disappear. The crowd looked around in puzzlement, and a marshal checked that the ball hadn't dropped on the fly into the hole. It hadn't, but the marshal moved the pin and the ball dropped to the ground just a couple of inches from the cup. The ball had hit the flag and wrapped itself up, suspended above the ground. Locke made his birdie.

"Honestly, Dad, you haven't given Steven and me any pocket money since 1987."

Old Elephant Dick
Hole still causing
problems - but
Chris looks happy
enough.

Tommy Armour

"Golf is an awkward set of **bodily** contortions designed to produce a graceful result."

Jones?

Every year in Tennessee there is a tournament held called the Bobby Jones Open. The only condition of entry is that a player must have the name Bobby Jones.

Let's dance

For the 1938 film Carefree, Fred Astaire tap danced his way down a row of 12 balls teed up at the driving range and hit each one with a driver, while still dancing. The scene was done in one continuous take, and Astaire made a clean contact with each ball - so clean that they all landed within eight feet of each other.

Suited up

Harry Dearth once played a round of golf at Bushey Hall GC while wearing a full suit of armour. He lost his match, 2&1.

"Yeah, you're right, I shouldn't have used a putter from in there".

Don't spend it all at once

They say that patience is eventually rewarded, but sometimes you have to wonder if it was really worth the wait. American player Becky Larson played five years on the LPGA Tour but didn't even come close to carving out a living. During those years, a run of 88 tournaments, Larson did not make a single cent in winnings. Her cashless streak finally came to an end in 1990 when she won $283 for finishing third from last at the Rail Charity Classic.

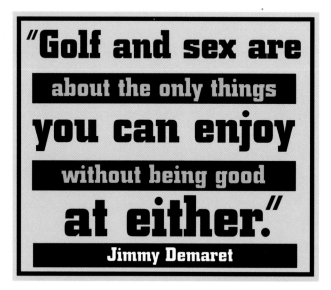

"Golf and sex are about the only things you can enjoy without being good at either."
Jimmy Demaret

Cross country

Two St Andrews University students fought out a bizarre golf match in 1938. They teed off at Ceres, a village some nine miles from the Old Course at St Andrews, where the 18th green was their intended destination. It took around eight hours to complete the "hole" and the winning margin was a narrow one, 236 strokes to 238.

Putt, putt

In 1939, a London stockbroker won a wager of £100 to golf his way, in less than 200 shots, across London from Tower Bridge to White's Club on St James's Street. He completed the route in a mere 142 shots, using only a putter.

"Ello, Momma! Guessa wot your bambino Costantino hasa won for you - a bigga cup to putta the pasta in..."

"The average golfer doesn't play golf. He attacks it." Jackie Burke

Orville's
honours

American professional golfer Orville Moody, playing for a few dollars against the locals of Bowie Country Club in Texas, had one of those days when everything goes right. He won the money with ease, taking just 57 strokes to play the par-72 course. The banter in the bar afterwards maintained that Moody had been lucky on his way round, a charge he was not willing to listen to for too long. "Let's go back out and I'll show you again" he told the barflies, and he then played the next nine holes in just 30 strokes - enough to convince the doubters that it was judgement more than luck on the day.

Never mind, eh?

The 1937 Amateur Championship was a tale of mammoth but ultimately futile journeys. Brigadier-General Critchley travelled from New York to Southampton by sea on the Queen Mary but was delayed by fog. He chartered a light aircraft to fly him directly to Sandwich for the tournament, and even circled the clubhouse to alert officials to his arrival. Unfortunately he still arrived six minutes past his allotted time and was struck from the tournament. Another player began his journey in Burma, voyaged across the Pacific and then the land mass of the USA to catch the same Queen Mary voyage only to arrive at the course four hours too late to compete.

What's in a name?

The trophy cabinet of Mrs Anne Sander must take some explaining to visitors: she has won four major amateur titles in her career, each under a different name. It started as Miss Quast with the 1958 US Ladies Amateur title; she won it again in 1961 as Mrs Decker, and then again in 1963 as Mrs Welts. Then in 1980 she won the British Ladies as Mrs Sander.

Snow
golf

The most southerly recorded golf course is the Scott Base Country Club at the South Pole. Some interesting local rules apply: if a ball is stolen by a skua, a one shot penalty is incurred. However, if the ball actually hits a skua, a birdie is recorded on the card.

Joe Pesci is a goodfella when he plays golf - so you always let him win.

"If some players took a **fork** to their mouths the way they take the club back they'd starve to death."

Sam Snead

"Samual L Jackson is the only one of us three who hasn't made a career out of falling down".

"I was in a film called Falling Down and you're always drunk. Geddit?"

Well, you would, wouldn't you?

Pennsylvania State College student Jason Bohn took part in a charity hole-in-one competition in Alabama in 1992. Twelve players each had one attempt to hole out from 135 yards with the prize of $1 million being given to whoever managed the feat. Bohn aced his only shot and promptly renounced his amateur status in return for a payment of $5,000 a month for 20 years.

Easy game

In 1907, John Ball took on a bet to play 18 holes at Hoylake, in less than 90 shots, in dense fog, in less than two and a quarter hours and without losing a ball. Ball managed to shoot 81 in the allotted time using a black ball all the way round.

Life, death and golf

So why was Mary Queen of Scots beheaded in 1857? One of the reasons stated at her trail was her display of complete indifference to the murder of her husband, Darnley. Instead of mourning suitably, Mary was seen to be playing golf in the fields of Seton just a few days after his death.

The mighty fall

The 1991 Open Champion Ian Baker-Finch found life a little tough just a few years on from his fabulous victory at Birkdale. In 1995 he entered 18 tournaments on the USPGA Tour and failed to make the cut in all of them. He therefore didn't earn a penny in winnings.

Two grand a yard

Robert Allenby earned a £75,000 bonus for hitting just one shot in the 1996 Volvo Masters. Allenby was still recovering from a broken sternum following a car accident, but to collect the bonus and preserve his position in the Order of Merit, the rules said he had to compete. The Australian duly turned up, managed to hit a drive 40 yards, and promptly withdrew. He donated the bonus to charity.

Mad for it

During 24 hours of daylight at the world's most northerly golf course, the Akureyri Club in Iceland, four British golfers completed 14 rounds of golf to raise money for charity.

In the money

Dale Larson caught his golf shoe spikes on the steps of the club bar at Indianhead GC in Wisconsin and fell over - breaking his jaw and several teeth. Larson was not sober at the time, in fact his blood-alcohol level suggested he was close to comatose. Nevertheless he sued the golf club and won over $50,000 in damages.

Go on, back a bit.

You're
nicked

New York cop Stan Garrant decided to stop by his local course on the way home from work for a quick game of golf. The pro told him he could join up with a threeball just about to set out. Garrant walked up to the tee, where his three new partners were sharing a cigarette - only it turned out to be marijuana. Garrant identified himself to the threesome, and then arrested them.

Lucky
stake

Roger Maltbie won the 1976 Memorial tournament thanks to a stroke of luck. Contesting a play-off with Hale Irwin, Maltbie hit a drive that was heading way off the course until it hit an out of bounds stake and flew back into play. Not surprisingly, Maltbie went on to win the play-off, and he then pulled the stake from the ground and carried it in his golf bag for good luck for the remainder of the season.

Tiger liked the cart so much he bought the TV company.

Cool nude

Jose Maria Olazabal is young, good looking and Spanish. Which is probably why in the 1991 Open Championship a 16-year-old blonde, female spectator decided to shed all her clothes and run over to the player and give him a big hug. Said Ollie afterwards: "It was just a naked woman, that's all."

Door trouble

Sam Torrance has a habit of finding himself in bizarre situations, but one of the worst was probably in Nice in 1991 when Sam returned to his hotel room after a day's work on the course. It was a lovely evening, so Sam decided to sit out on his balcony - in the nude. Then a gust of wind blew the balcony door shut, leaving Torrance locked outside, with no clothes. As the sun went down, Torrance began to feel the cold. After 45 minutes he managed to attract a passer-by's attention who then sent help up to his room.

He's got bottle

In the days before he tasted success on the professional Tour, Lee Trevino used to scrape a living together playing golf games for money. For a period of time this involved taking on players around a 9-hole pitch and putt course with Trevino using only a large fizzy drink bottle wrapped in tape - he invariably broke 30 for the nine holes.

Not a bad living

At the age of 20, while still attending college, Jack Nicklaus was given a special dispensation to sell insurance to help finance his amateur golf exploits. Normally to sell insurance in Ohio a person had to be 21. The Golden Bear to be raked in about $25,000 in earnings while still a student.

Isao Aoki meditating - I can play golf.....I can play golf...

And this was
just the first
hole.

What a way to meet

Dinah Oxley paid a heavy price for hitting a wild drive at Alwoodley in Leeds. Her ball flew out of bounds and onto an adjacent road, where it smashed the windscreen of an oncoming car. The car was driven by James Henson, who immediately pulled over. Ms Oxley invited Henson to the clubhouse for a cup of tea to calm his nerves. They chatted and got on well. They eventually married.

> The game just embarrasses you until you feel inadequate and pathetic. You want to cry like a child
>
> Craig Stadler

Intimidatory tactics

Leading the 1985 Milwaukee Open by three shots from Jack Nicklaus, Jim Thorpe was subjected to a little gamesmanship from Nicklaus as they strode up the final fairway. Nicklaus asked Thorpe: "How does it feel to be walking down the last fairway with a three shot lead over the greatest player the game has ever known?"

To which Thorpe shot back: "It feels like you can't win."

CRAZY GOLF!

Let's...

...twist

...again

Not his favourite course

Dave Hill finished runner-up to Tony Jacklin in the 1970 US Open, but he was no fan of the Hazeltine venue. In one press interview he said: "If I had to play this course every day for fun, I'd find me another game."

When asked what the course lacked, Hill commented: "Eighty acres of corn and a few cows. They ruined a good farm when they built this course."

Thoughts of Herman

Herman Mitchell is a giant of a man, and a celebrity in his own right - he has served for many years as caddie to Lee Trevino. On one occasion Trevino was unsure of the line of a putt and asked Herman what he thought. The big man looked at the line and then told his boss: "Keep it low."

Can I have my ball back, please?

A visitor to the Eden course at St Andrews in 1955 saw his opening tee shot slice towards a train heading north on the railway track which runs alongside the course. The ball flew through an open window of one of the carriages, from where it was thrown back on to the fairway by a passenger who waved to the golfer as he went past.

He double
bogied the
hole.

"Golf is a game
where white men
can **dress up** as
pimps and get
away with it."
Robin Williams

Gerald Ford

"I know I'm getting better at golf because I hit fewer spectators."

Keep your hands to yourself

In the 1973 Heritage Classic, Hale Irwin hit a shot off target which struck a woman in the gallery, sneaked under her shirt and found refuge in her bra. Irwin was allowed under the rules of golf to remove the ball and drop without penalty, but the woman felt it best that she undertook the first part of the operation.

Big Bill

Not many golfers in the world can boast achieving an albatross - playing a hole in 3-under its par. Big hitting Bill Graham could probably top any albatross story in the bar after a game, he made a two at the 16th hole at Whiting Field in Florida. Graham hit driver and then holed his 3-wood second shot - the hole measured 602 yards.

Harsh but true

After the third round of the 1976 Masters, Ray Floyd led Jack Nicklaus by eight shots and Larry Ziegler by nine. A reporter asked Ziegler what he thought he would have to shoot the following day to have any chance of winning. He replied: "Floyd."

Golden Bear
valiantly trying
to stretch out
his career.

Watch
your mouth

The Masters is a unique Championship in that it is organised and run by the committee of Augusta National, the one and only Masters venue. To such an extent that they can even influence the TV coverage. So when CBS broadcaster Jack Whitaker referred on air to the gallery as a "teeming mob" instead of the preferred terminology of "patrons" - he was barred from commentating on The Masters again.

Gary McCord is another who has felt the wrath of Augusta - when he commented that the slope from the 15th green down to the creek in front was so short and fast that they must have used bikini wax on it, he too was ejected and banned from future TV participation.

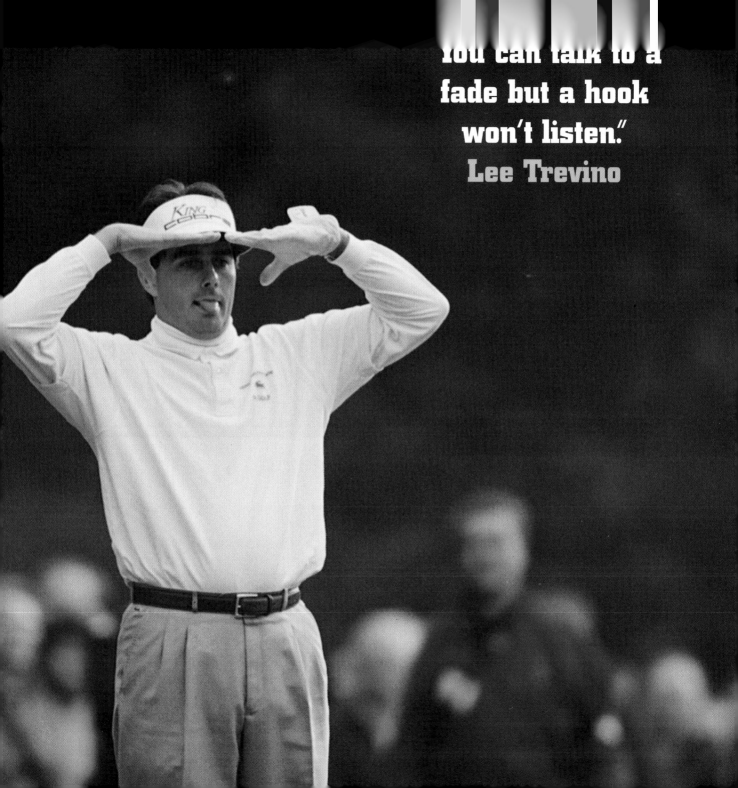

You can talk to a fade but a hook won't listen."
Lee Trevino

Stupido

Seve Ballesteros never had much of a happy time at the US Open. Straight driving has never been a strong point in his game, and the penalties for hitting the rough in the US Open are severe to say the least. In the 1980 Championship, Ballesteros opened with a 75 to lie 12 shots behind the leaders. The next day was an even bigger nightmare. Staying just a 10 minute drive from the course, Seve set out at 9.25am for a 10am tee-time. Unfortunately, his tee-off was actually 9.45am, and to add to that he got stuck in traffic. When he arrived at the course he was too late to catch his playing partners up, and he was disqualified. He said afterwards: "I am a stupido. Now I'm embarrassed. I came all this way for nothing."

Wrong turn

Fiji entered a team for the 1980 World Amateur Championships scheduled for Pinehurst, North Carolina. The nearest airport is Fayetteville, and as the plane started its landing preparations, the Fijian team changed into national dress for the welcoming party. Unfortunately, the plane landed in Fayetteville, Arkansas, where the temperature was a lot lower than in North Carolina.

Can't trust anyone these days

For the 1991 British Amateur Championship, the R&A, the governing body of golf and organiser of the tournament, decided to lay on practice balls for the competitors, and purchased 1,008, brand spanking new, balata balls for the players to use on the range. By the end of the week, every single one of the balls had disappeared, stolen by the competitors.

What to do?

1969 Masters Champion George Archer couldn't figure what to do with his retirement. He opined: "Baseball players quit playing and take up golf. Basketball players quit and take up golf. Football players quit and take up golf. What are we supposed to take up when we quit?"

Toilet trouble

For the 1981 US Open, Jack Nicklaus complained that the toilet facilities for players on the course were not up to scratch. So the organisers decided to move a couple of toilet cabins from the spectators side of the ropes to a place where they were exclusively for players. As a forklift hoisted one of the cabins into the air, a scream emerged from within, the door flew open and there sat a woman, in some distress. The forklift put her down gently on the ground, and workers waited while she finished her business, and walked off with as much dignity as she was able to pull together in the circumstances.

"Colin Montgomerie has a face like a warthog that has been stung by a wasp." David Feherty

"When it blows here, even the seagulls walk." Nick Faldo on St Andrews

Payne Stewart trying the John Daly approach to golf.

"Never bet with anyone you meet on the 1st tee who has a deep suntan, a 1-iron in his bag and squinty eyes." Dave Marr

I've seen you play an air shot before, but not a bloody moon shot!

Four!

Scottish professional Ben Sayers once won a bet against an American tourist who wagered that Sayers could not go round and score a four at each and every one of the 18 holes. Sayers did so.

Doh!

Hale Irwin never won the Open Championship, but he came very close. In 1983 he finished second, just a shot behind Tom Watson. And that shot only measured a couple of inches. On the 14th green during the 3rd round, Irwin knocked his approach shot stiff, just inches from the hole. When he went to casually tap the putt in, however, he missed the ball completely. His putter struck the ground before the ball and bounced straight over it, meaning he made five instead of four.

The bridesmaid

Tom Weiskopf was widely acknowledged as having one of the best swings in professional golf, but it only ever brought him one Major title, the Open Championship. In later life he turned to TV commentary and was behind the microphone as Jack Nicklaus stormed to victory at the 1986 Masters. As Nicklaus lined up a crucial putt at the 16th, a fellow broadcaster asked Weiskopf what he thought was in Nicklaus' mind at the time. Weiskopf replied: "If I knew I would have won this golf tournament." The best Weiskopf did in The Masters was runner-up - on four occasions.

Good tackle

Playing the 1985 Open Championship, Peter Jacobsen prepared to chip to the last green when he saw a male streaker emerge from the crowd and head directly towards the green. Jacobsen reacted quickly, and felled the streaker with a perfectly timed tackle. Jacobsen explained his actions afterwards: "He was about to run across the line of my shot. I put my shoulder in where it hurts most."

The dole queue beckons

Bill Kratzert had no reason to thank his caddie at the 1986 Anheuser-Busch Classic. A steaming hot July day, Kratzert's caddie decided to lighten his load as much as possible, and emptied his employer's golf bag of all but three golf balls. The load got even lighter as Kratzert put on a display of wild hitting, and pretty soon his meagre supply of ammunition was exhausted - and he had to withdraw from the tournament.

Stick to grass greens Laura.

Greedy tree

Maintenance men trimming a huge cypress tree at San Francisco's Olympic Club in 1977 got something of a surprise when they started shaking the tree around. Out fell 105 golf balls it had plucked from the air and held on to.

> "If you're going to throw a club, it's important to throw it ahead of you, down the fairway, so you don't waste energy going back to pick it up."
>
> Tommy Bolt

Friends

Sandy Lyle and Nick Faldo fell out big time at the Kenyan Open early on their pro careers. Lyle was blinded by the glare of the sun off his putter head as prepared to putt, so he solved the problem by placing a sticking plaster along the top edge to stop the reflection. Faldo reported Lyle for infringing the rules, and the Scotsman was disqualified.

Late lunch

Slow play was a problem at the 1991 US Women's Open, with rounds lasting beyond five hours in exhausting heat. Lori Garbacz showed some initiative when her group was held up yet again - she somehow got a message to a local pizza delivery company and they served her and her playing partners a delicious pizza on the 17th tee.

Helping foot

Contesting the 1923 PGA Championship final, Walter Hagen found that local boy Gene Sarazen was in receipt of some partisan support. Approaching the 14th green, which was guarded by water, Sarazen hit his lay up shot too long and the ball seemed destined to roll into the water. Until a boy in a red sweater emerged and stopped the ball with his foot, saving Sarazen the hole. Sarazen went on to win the Championship in a play-off.

Costly miss

Leo Diegel could have won the 1933 Open Championship, but for the fact he found putting such a painful part of the game. As Diegel came to the final green of the Championship, he needed to take just two putts to win the title. He lagged his first putt close to the hole, but then completely missed the ball when trying to make the tap-in.

Fuzzy Zoeller

"Seve Ballesteros drives into territory even **Daniel Boone** couldn't find."

David Beckham taking a dive... sorry, driver to the ball.

Mine's a pint

The 18th green at Moortown GC in Leeds is only a matter of yards from the clubhouse, as Nigel Denham found when playing in the 1974 English Amateur. His approach shot overshot the green, bounced on the pathway, and disappeared through an open door into the clubhouse bar.

The ball was technically still in play, and Denham was faced with a shot from the bar to the green, which he could see through the window. He opened the window, chipped the ball off the carpet, through the window and onto the green. Amazingly, he then sank the putt and walked off with a par.

Sandy grave

The tiny 8th hole at Royal Troon, a mere 120 yards long, has claimed many victims. One of the worst was German pro Herman Tissies during the 1950 Open Championship. Tissies bunkered his tee shot, and then played from bunker to another - and actually took five attempts in one of them. When he finally got onto the green he three-putted for a 15.

I said I'm not very good with numbers.

Help from a greater force

In May 1932, a golfer playing in Mexico City hit his tee shot at a par-3 to the very edge of the hole, a whisker from a hole in one. At that moment, the city was hit by an earthquake, and before the player could take his putt for a two, the ball was tipped into the hole by the tremors from below.

He's really pylon the pressure.

Bob Hope is in Heaven.

Load of
bull

Golf equipment is a fertile ground for inventors, and many daft ideas have been submitted to the patent office for protection. Take for example the golf ball developed by W Langstaff in 1912. Langstaff's revolutionary new material for the core of the ball was nothing other than a bull's penis.

Hitting the bottle

In the 1949 Open Championship, Harry Bradshaw found his ball had come to rest inside a broken glass bottle. Unsure as to the rules, Bradshaw played the ball as it lay, managing to move it 30-odd yards down the fairway, but he ended the hole with a double bogey 6. Come the end of the tournament, Bradshaw was tied for the lead but lost in a play-off.

Jones' stones

In the 1930s, Bobby Jones made a trip to Europe and played a golf course situated in a forest near Budapest. To mark the occasion, the locals placed a white stone exactly where each of Jones' drives had landed in the course of his round.

Golf in Bari, Italy, is a banned sport on Sundays– even though there is no golf course in the town.

Justin signing autographs after he made a cut.

Golf fashion is a bit outlandish, but the bloke in the middle takes the biscuit.

WELLS FARGO

Top blagger

The 1980 US Open was the scene of a rather opportunistic piece of gate crashing when 7-handicapper Barry Bremen managed to bluff his way on to the practice ground saying he was a competitor. He then joined up with another group out on the course for a practice game and completed the round before officials realised they had been duped.

David Feherty

"The only time Nick Faldo opens his mouth is to change feet."

Cheats never prosper

Charles Carey played in a charity tournament in Indiana in 1993, and returned a score of 67. Unfortunately, plain clothes detectives, acting on a tip-off, had kept an eye on Carey on the way round, and figured he had actually shot 80, so they arrested him for theft of his prize of a $50 gift voucher.

Cool Green

Hubert Green won the 1977 US Open, but he played the last few holes of the Championship in the knowledge that the police had received a death threat against him. Green joked that it was probably an ex-girlfriend who had made the threat.

Jose-Maria obviously lost the bet with the Barber of Seville.

Tiger liked the bridge so much, he bought the golf course for his mates.

Early bird

Getting disqualified for being late on the tee is a fairly common experience. Being disqualified for teeing off early is not. But Ed Oliver was denied a play-off place in the 1940 US Open for starting his final round too early. He and five other players made an early start because of a grim weather forecast - all were disqualified on completion of the round. Oliver's total of 287 would have put him in a play-off with Gene Sarazen and Lawson Little.

Night shift

Ray Floyd, four-time Major winner and a one-time Ryder Cup captain, once managed a topless all-girl band called The Ladybirds. Lightning strike Lee Trevino was one of three players struck by lightning during the 1975 Western Open. Trevino said afterwards: "There was this thunderous crack like cannonfire and suddenly I was lifted a foot and a half off the ground. Damn it, I thought to myself, this is one helluva penalty for slow play."

Only fair

During the war at Richmond GC a local rule was introduced that allowed a player to play another ball under penalty of one stroke should his shot be affected by the simultaneous explosion of a bomb.

Clumsy caddie

The 1946 US Open featured great crowds, but unfortunately not many marshals. At the 13th hole the crowd was so big that when Eddie Martin, caddie for Byron Nelson, finally stumbled through the ropes, he inadvertently trod on his master's ball. Nelson had to incur a penalty, and it ultimately cost him the title as he had to compete in a play-off which he lost to Lloyd Mangrum.

A Tiger Woods approach shot to the green.

Dan Jenkins

"A good **1-iron shot** is about as easy to come by as an understanding wife."

"Hey, Pesci, put that cigar out."

"Shut it, Lemmon, or I'll stick it up your ass".

Magic carpet

With water being a scarce product in South Yemen, so is grass. Not that the rich owners of one course in Habban mind, they have a solution which allows them to produce perfect surfaces for golf - they laid lush, green carpet.

Cry baby

Arnold Palmer wears contact lenses these days while playing golf. Sometimes on windy days they dry out and he has to lubricate them, a feat he achieves mid-round by forcing himself to cry - "I just think about my putting," said Palmer.

Tree trouble

Bob Hope knows a thing about playing golf with US Presidents, he has, after all, partnered five of them. The biggest snag to it is, apparently, the multitude of secret service agents who accompany the President on any trip. Says Hope: "When you hit a ball, the trees get up and run along beside you."

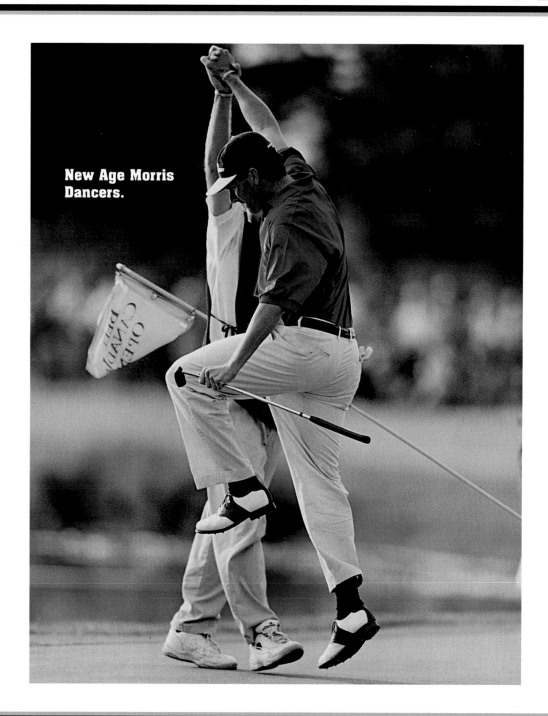

New Age Morris
Dancers.

Almost
cleaned
out

For winning the 1970 US Open, Tony Jacklin received a cheque for $30,000, which he folded and put in his jacket pocket, and then forgot about. When he got home he sent his suit to be cleaned, and luckily the cleaner found the cheque in the pocket.

Just in case

Harry Vardon, six times Open Champion, apparently used to carry one left handed club in his bag just in case he found his normal stance hindered by a tree or bush.

> "Being left-handed is a big advantage. No-one knows enough about your swing to mess you up with advice."
>
> Bob Charles

Damon Hill with a text book swing, which text book we haven't quite figured out yet.

In the dark

Seve Ballesteros and Bernhard Langer had to share the 1986 Lancome Trophy due to the fact that falling darkness meant it was not possible to continue the head to head play-off beyond four holes.

Ooh er!

"Ladies are allowed to play the course in trousers, but are requested to remove them before they enter the clubhouse." A sign at Royal St George's - circa 1946.

Must try harder

John Daly, no stranger to controversy, set a new US Tour record in 1998 at the Bay Hill Invitational tournament. Daly managed to find the water seven times off the tee of a par-5 hole and managed to end up taking an 18. "I was trying with every one. I tried to stay patient but I guess I just lost it," he said afterwards.

David Feherty

"When John Daly hits an iron, he takes a cubic yard of Kent as well. His **divots** go further than my drives."

Power player

Kurt Durst of Stuttgart once managed to short out the power supply for whole swathes of his home town. Practising his swing, Durst inadvertently let go of the club and it struck an overhead power line, cutting supply for over three hours.

"Go on, make my day ball."

Careful, lads, Jesper uses volcanic dust to cleanse his system.

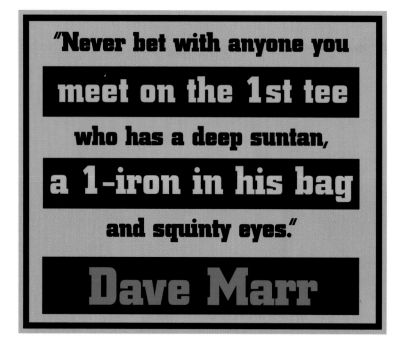

"Never bet with anyone you meet on the 1st tee who has a deep suntan, a 1-iron in his bag and squinty eyes."

Dave Marr

Calm on the outside

"Don't throw up. Not now. Hang on for 10 more minutes." The thought process of Davis Love III as told to John Feinstein in "A Good Walk Spoiled" as Love III nears Ryder Cup victory against Costantino Rocca in 1993.

Be warned

"Trespassers may be eaten" - a warning sign to golfers who might try and retrieve errant drives at Sandown zoo, alongside the golf course.

Look out! It's behind you.

Time changes man

Lee Trevino on his game in his 20s, and the game he plays today: "I still swing the way I used to, but when I look up the ball is going in a different direction."

"Seve is a genius, one of the few true geniuses of the game. The thing is, Seve is never in trouble. He's in the trees quite a lot, but that's not trouble for him. That's normal."
Ben Crenshaw

The toilet facilities at some golf courses leaves a lot to be desired... let alone what passes for toilet paper.

Amazing Adrian

Adrian Donkersley, playing at Little Chalfont, had a dream stretch between the 9th and 14th. His scores progressed: 6, 5, 4, 3, 2, 1 - level par for the six holes.

Moving target

The par-3 14th hole at the Coeur d'Alene golf course in Idaho features a floating, island green. What's more it can be moved - so the hole can measure anything from 75 yards to 175.

"If Jack Nicklaus had to play my tee shots he couldn't break 80. He'd be a pharmacist with a string of drug stores in Ohio."
Lee Trevino

Spaniard
sunk

Young Spaniard Ignacio Garrido played his first ever Masters in 1998, but didn't make the most auspicious of starts. He opened with a round of 86, which included a tournament record equalling 15 on the par-5 15th hole. Garrido visited the water three times and then, to add insult to injury, three-putted.

Easy five,
really

In the 1981 B&H tournament at Fulford, Bernhard Langer's shot to the 17th green hit a tree and stayed in its branches. Langer climbed up the tree, and clipped the ball free from the branches to the green, and scrambled off with a five.

"She's hit one"!

That was a Payne-ful shot.

"The slums
of Chicago
are full of
first round
leaders."
Payne Stewart

"Competitive
golf is played
mainly on a
five and a
half inch
course -
the space
between your
ears."
Bobby Jones

Dan Jenkins

"**Golfers** don't fist fight.

They cuss a bit. But they wouldn't punch anything or anybody. They might **hurt** their hands and have to change their grip."

"My old name was fine for a violin player but lousy for a golfer."

Gene Sarazen,
formerly Eugene Saraceni

"A long drive is good for the ego".
Arnold Palmer

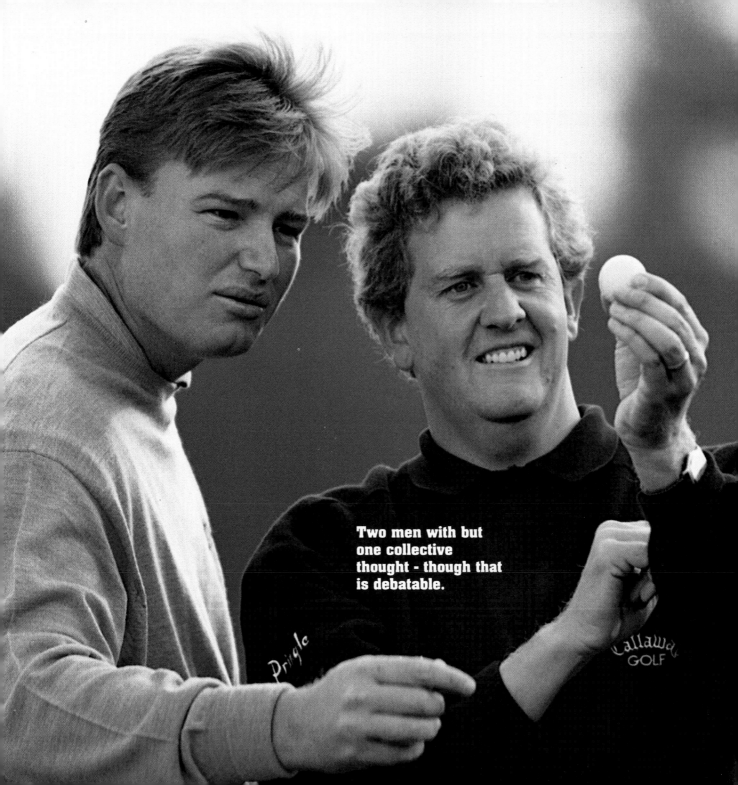

Two men with but
one collective
thought - though that
is debatable.

"I go anywhere they know me. I go to Japan, they know me. I never see a player miss a putt and become so famous. I just miss a putt. I don't kill nobody."

Costantino Rocca reflects on a missed putt that let the USA in to win the 1993 Ryder Cup.

"I was swinging like a

toilet door

on a prawn trawler."

David Feherty

after a bad day

If only your
swing was as
cool, Samuel.

"His driving is unbelievable.
I don't go that far on my holidays."
Ian Baker-Finch on John Daly

Yes... they've even given Fergie a TV programme, and they've called it Surviving Life.

"MY WORST DAY
ON THE GOLF COURSE
STILL BEATS
MY BEST DAY IN THE
OFFICE"
JOHN HALLISEY

"My swing is so bad I look like a caveman killing his lunch."
Lee Trevino

We know what you're
doing.

"I can't swing the way I want to
with four sweaters and my
pyjamas and a rain jacket on."

Lee Trevino playing in Scotland

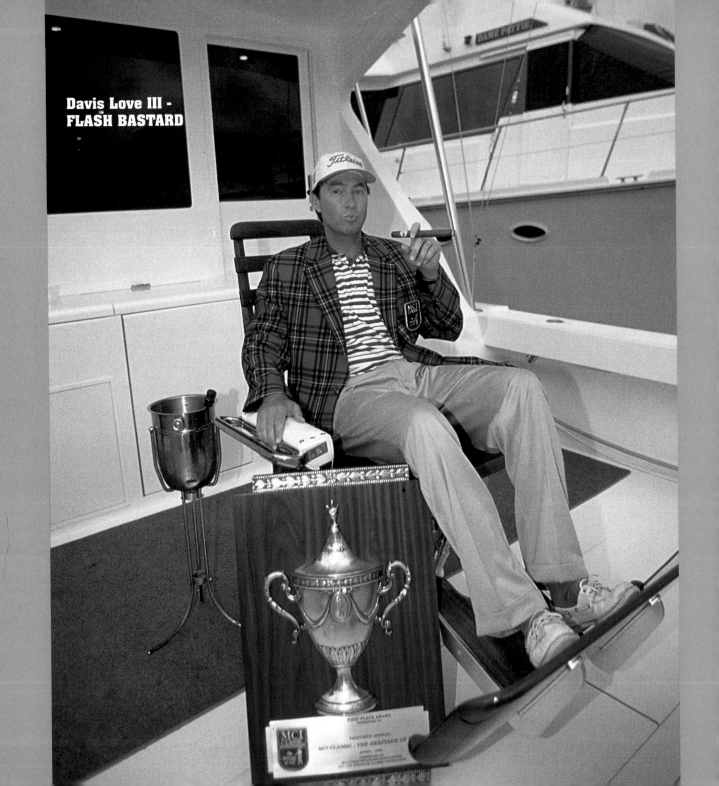

Davis Love III -
FLASH BASTARD

Golf giveth and golf taketh away. But it taketh away a hell of a lot more than it giveth."
Simon Hobday

"Golf is the most fun you can have without taking your clothes off."
Chi Chi Rodriguez

"You know he's gonna beat you. He knows he's gonna beat you. And he knows you know he's gonna beat you."
Leonard Thompson on Jack Nicklaus

"Some guys get so nervous playing for their own money, the greens don't need fertilising for a year." **Dave Hill**

"I don't say my golf game is bad, but if I grew **tomatoes** they'd come up sliced."

Miller Barber

"They should put down the knife and fork a bit more often." **Gary Player** passes comment on **Lee Westwood** and **Darren Clarke**

"There's nothing wrong with the Old Course at St Andrews that **100 bulldozers** couldn't put right. The Old Course needs a dry clean and press." **Ed Furgol**

Denis Law, Scottish footballer supreme, admitted to being on a golf course when **England** were winning the **World Cup in 1966.**

This man single-handedly tried to put the fashion back in golf...

he failed miserably.

Look, Samuel, own up,
you re a crap golfer whoever
your mates are.

"I'm about **five inches** from being an
outstanding golfer. That's the distance my left
ear is from my right." Ben Crenshaw

"Jose-Maria, you've got to lay off that bean soup."

"I would like to deny all allegations by **Bob Hope** that during my last game **I hit an eagle,** a birdie, an elk and a **moose.**"

Gerald Ford

"Golf balls are attracted to water as unerringly as the eye of a middle aged man to a female bosom."

Michael Green

"My wife always said she wanted to marry a millionaire. Well, she married a millionaire. I used to be a multi-millionaire." Lee Trevino

"Not like something from Scotland or Ireland, it's like something from **Mars**." David Feherty on Kiawah Island, venue for the Ryder Cup in 1991.

John Daly resting between holes.

"Golf is a game in which a ball - one and half inches in diameter - is placed on a ball - 8,000 miles in diameter. The object being to hit the small ball but not the larger."

John Cunningham

"Nobody but you and your caddie care what you do out there, and if your caddie is betting against you, he doesn't care either."

Lee Trevino

"You know he's gonna beat you. He knows he's gonna beat you. And he knows you know he's gonna beat you."

Leonard Thompson on Jack Nicklaus

IF YOU ENJOYED THIS BOOK, WHAT ABOUT THESE!

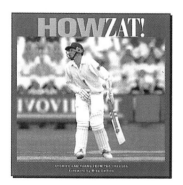

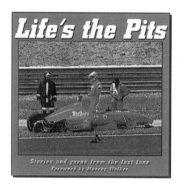

All these books are available at your local bookshop or can be ordered direct from the publisher.
Just list the titles you require and give your name address, including postcode.
Prices and availability are subject to change without notice.

Please send to Chameleon Cash Sales, 76 Dean Street, London W1V 5HA, a cheque or postal
order for £7.99 and add the following for postage and packaging:
UK - £1.00 For the first book, 50p for the second and 30p for the third and for each additional
book up to a maximum of £3.00.
OVERSEAS - (including Eire) £2.00 For the first book, £1.00 for the second and 50p for each
additional book up to a maximum of £3.00.